Life is a terrible thing to waste and time is irreplaceable.

A Precious Gift From God

*Absolutely Non- Refundable,
Paid in full with the Blood of
Jesus the Christ*

Parice C. Parker

<u>*Life is a terrible thing to waste and time is irreplaceable.*</u>

A Precious Gift from God

Published by Fountain of Life Publisher's House

P. O. Box 922612 Norcross, GA 30010
Phone: 404-936-3989
Please Email Manuscripts to: publish@pariceparker.biz
For all book orders including wholesale email: sales@pariceparker.biz
To request author email: author@pariceparker.biz
www.pariceparker.biz

Fountain of Life Publishing House is committed to excellence in the publishing industry. The Company reflects the philosophy established by the founder, based on Psalm 68:11, *"The Lord gave the word and great was the company of those who published it."*

Cover Design by Parice Parker
Interior design by Parice C. Parker
Editor: Phyllis R. Brown

Published in the United States of America

ISBN: ***0-9787162-5-6***
3.16.16

Life is a terrible thing to waste and time is irreplaceable.

A Precious Gift From God

Table of Contents

Chapters

Parice C. Parker

<u>*Life is a terrible thing to waste and time is irreplaceable.*</u>

Introduction:

Just when you think you have forgotten, and needing fulfillment, God will present you with a very special gift. A gift is typically given to you by surprise. An award is given to uplift, encourage, and packed with love. A gift from God should always appreciated because it is priceless. God worked miraculously, just to give you, and me the most precious divine gift of all. You will never know what all God has packed in this Gift. Unwrap it, and receive it with gladness in your heart. This gift is non-refundable and packed with shipping power from The Most High. It is The Anointed at large! Assuredly, it's powered directly from Heaven to you. This gift is the most valuable gift you will ever receive. So, therefore, enjoy this opportunity, and unwrap your gift. This gift is perfect.

Parice C. Parker

A Precious Gift From God

"If today was your last day on your job, how prepared would you be?"

Parice C. Parker

Chapter One
Identify Your Gift

There are so many reasons that God gives us gifts. Your gift may come through a celebration or special occasion. He always knows how to keep our hearts stayed on Him. Most people recognize their gifts during a terrible storm, or when something traumatic happens. He always brings forth our gifts during our most needed times. I remember when I first recognized one of my gifts. I was so angry with the way my life was; I just began to write. The many temptations that tried to tempt me, I resisted them as I heavily endured. As my anguish was still building, I could only release it to a pen and a piece of paper. Once I finished writing, I read it aloud and I could not stop! It came to be my first book, "Aggravated Assault on Your Mind." I realized God's purpose was to make us feel special during our most trying times. It is something how He gives us gifts. However, each time God gave me a gift was the time I most needed to be strengthened. God has a tremendous way of surprising us. 2 Samuel 22:40 says, For Thou has girded me with strength to battle: them that rose up against me hast thou subdued under my feet. Your gift will be your power to overcome once you recognize how valuable it is. There is so much power in your gift that it will cause you to win all your battles, even before your campaign appears. Just like David, he was one that was extremely gifted in many ways, from being one of the greatest inspirational writers of all times, until he was able to inspire His Lord of Lords and Kings of Kings. His gifts caused heaven to keep him covered. God is mighty, and He owns the fortress of true happiness. He owns every good deed, every true conqueror and knows every life destiny. There was one occasion when I wanted to turn back. I begin to grow tired in trying to accomplish. It seemed the more I was praying and seeking the worst my life appeared. The more I went to church the higher my mountains grew and the more I testified, the more my life seemed to fall. I begin to ask myself, "Why, why, why should I continue living right and everything else is going so wrong?" It just seemed that I was more blessed when I used to live in the world. However, a voice said to me, "Utilize Your Gifts!" The truth was right there in my hearing, and I know that it was The Holy Spirit speaking to me. At that moment, I was so angry I begin to write out my feelings. I opened my heart to a piece of paper and allowed the pen to have its way. Then I read it aloud; it was remarkable, and instantly I felt so much better. As I read what I had written out of my heart, I realized that it was not I, but it was God writing through me. Ever since then, I begin to write. I realized God gave me the gift of writing to keep my mind focused on Him. He wants us to speak to Him with our gifts. He wants to be inspired; that is why David was the apple of his eye.

David took the time to inspire God. Many of us are so busy going to God for our needs, that we don't take the time to encourage heaven to begin a work on our behalf. Our gifts are absolute, non-refundable – it's His heart. God has wrapped His heart in this Gift, and it will bring you joy during your times of sorrow. Your gift is to inspire you well as heaven, no matter what you are going through. Jesus will gain greater recognition through the utilization of appreciating your gift. We all have many types of gifts, and your gift is unique. Our Heavenly Father wants to be inspired! I sometimes know it's hard for us to use our gifts during troubled times. Nevertheless, truly it's the best time for your gift to expand. It can be a marriage separation, a hard fall in life, a death or even some other unexpected life destruction. It does not matter; Jesus wants our sincere trust in Him. If you believe that Jesus is greater than any situation and circumstance, then you will begin to inspire Him, and He will change your position. He gives us gifts for a purpose, and He wants to be inspired. Understand there is drawing power in the utilization of your gift. First of all, it lets God know how much you appreciate Him. Secondly, it will cause someone else's burdens lifted. Besides, thirdly, it will cause someone to recognize Him for you. Every time you use your gift, someone will gain an opportunity to be encouraged. I believe within all of my heart that David pleased God, despite his sins. David only wanted God. Often many put their focus on their sin until they can't cause God to move. However, we all have fallen short at one time or another, and we should always continue to try trusting God more. The more we fall short, the more we shorten Jesus of receiving His glory. Romans 3:23 says, For all have sinned, and come short of the glory of God. There is only one way to overcome sin, and that is to keep on trying to please God. David's heart's desire was to satisfy God through His writings. Every song he sang testified of His God. David's greatest accomplishment is the Glory that he is still causing God to receive, even until this day. That is the same thing that God wants from you and me; that is to inspire Him. David simply knew how to motivate God, and he didn't stop until he did. Romans 12:6 says, Having then gifts differing according to the grace that is given to us, whether prophecy, let us prophesy according to the proportion of faith; David's faith was mighty in God because he knew how to anticipate God to move in his life. He was a believer in God's word, and his faith was proportioned well in Him. I mean absolutely nothing caused David to stop trying to please God - Surely no sin, no battle, circumstance or situation. His purpose was set in His mind to overcome, and He always gave God that Glory to be his burden carrier. He continuously inspired God! Understand your gift has been paid to you with a supernatural intention to develop something wonderful out of you. Once you recognize your gift, you need to seek the purpose of it. And you should not stop until God says, He is satisfied. For different reasons, God gives us gifts. No one could ever receive, respect and honor your gift as you can. Your gift was specially designed just for your life. Also, no one could appreciate it or utilize it as God would have you too. It has a purpose to fulfill your life with many wonderful things, as it will give God greater recognition. Truly, its primary objective is to inspire God. Often we are not prepared to accept our gifts in the manner God will give them to us. All the same, we do not understand how powerful our gifts will be in our lives, let alone someone else's. There were times I wanted to give up. Yes, I wanted to throw in the towel. However, my gifts saved me time and time again. When I realized the gift of writing was upon me, I begin to become more resistant to the enemy. Many times, being tempted I was driven to utilize my gifts. I begin to write books or music. The Holy Spirit wanted to develop God, and I enriched me. The writings were my inspiration. Not only did they inspire me, but I believe they too inspired God. As I wrote, the tension was released. My anger grew to calmness and peace would surrender me. My life was appointed to writing and as I wrote God delivered me. Your gift has a purpose to cause you to overcome. It does not matter what your gifts are, just utilize them. They will serve many great purposes in your life well as others. I Timothy 4:14 says, Neglect not the gift that is in thee, which was given thee by prophecy, with the laying on of the hands of the presbytery.

Often we are so caught up with our nothing of life until we simply neglect our gifts. Notice, every time you ignore your contributions, you also cause negligence to become the leader of your prosperity. Just think, once negligence is your life leader then so is a failure, bondage, corruption, dead works, no vision and no great rewards. Look upon your gift and notice its value. It is truly priceless. God wants you to utilize the gift(s) that He has given you because He wishes to bring you out of bondage. He wants you sitting high, and He wants everyone to look at you, and say, "Now he or she is more than a conqueror." When you step through any entrance, He wants many to notice that you are blessed and highly favored. Give others a reason to desire after righteousness; let them see God through you. Be the one that will cause a chain reaction, for people to seek God as though they have lost their minds.

Imagine if you had the position in life as God has, think of all the prayers, heart desires, needs, burdens, and so much more being put on Him daily. God instructs all that are heavy laden to come to Him. None of us could be Him, but just imagine all that you put on Him in your lifetime, less alone the whole world. All I know is that when

I'm inspired it will motivate me encourage my heart and make me feel incredibly special. And once I feel extremely special I smile, I glow, I run, and I become more than a conqueror. Your gift is to make you and to satisfy Him every time you utilize it. Allow Him to know that you appreciate your gift and no matter what use it. I remember during this particular conference I began to sing, and the people were amazed. It wasn't how I was singing, but it was the way I sung. I remember when I began singing people truly picked on me. However, I kept on singing. No one knew what I was going through or what The Lord was currently doing in my life. Nevertheless, when hell rises in your life allow your gift to raise you up in Jesus. I had never sung in that particular manner, until this conference. At the time, my life was going through the fire, and my voice was the way I testified. See, I just had a stroke at only 36, being partially paralyzed on my right side. Knowing The Truth, I did not let it stop me from praising my Lord. Praise The Lord I was healed. I utilized my gift(s) with a different heart desire and a deeper strength, from the bottom of my belly was my voice heard. One came up to me and said, "Sing Pastor Parker, sing." She said, "Yokes are destroyed, and burdens are lifted when you sing." I have never received such a powerful comment on my singing as that; to The Holy Spirit, I give The Glory. Your gift has the power to lose someone that is confined, to free someone from bondage, and to cause someone's hell to be denounced. You must recognize the power that is in your gift, and it doesn't matter who you are or even what you have done, utilize your gift(s). Now, what if I would have allowed the crucial comments of others throughout the years to hinder my progress? Though many laughed at me, they didn't understand all that I had gone through. I sing to be released; it's a way I praise and a way I'm freed. It is also a way I communicate with Jehovah. I realized that no matter what, people are going to criticize you whether you are doing good or bad. I have often thought that if I had kept my mouth shut because someone told me to, would God have been satisfied with me? No, I don't think God would not have been pleased with me. I didn't come to satisfy a man, but I am born to please my Glorious Creator. 1 John 4:4 says, Ye are of God, little children, and have overcome them: because greater is he that is in you, than he that is in the world.

There wasn't one battle that David could fight alone; he needed superhuman strength for every battle. He did not let anything or anyone stop him. His main purpose was to gain the heart of God. Understand that in gaining one's heart, you must try to reach for it. You will do all that is necessary to obtain the love you desire, by doing what you need to receive it. Nothing will stop you; not even sin will get in your way. That is why we can bend; God knew we would need to bow in forgiveness – over, and over again. Once He forgives you, it's done – so, therefore, move on. David knew that he would always overcome because He knew who He served. 2 Samuel 7:26 says, And let thy name be magnified forever, saying, The Lord of hosts is the God over Israel: and let the house of thy servant David be established before thee.

God has promised me so many wonderful things, what about you? Hold on to your promises, and His word, for they will never fail you. Remember the more you use your gifts, the more He will be acknowledged to be God in and through your life. Also, the more He is exalted through your gifts, the more He will be motivated to move in your life. So, therefore, recognize the power that is in your gift. Unwrap it, and show it to the world. Be proud of it, and let it be seen, heard and known until you inspire God. 1 John 4:4 says, Ye are of God, little children, and have overcome them:

because greater is he that is in you, than he that is in the world.

Chapter Two
Crank Up the Volume

When God speaks to you, know His voice. It is amazing, how the enemy will come in just to destroy you. He finds his way to sneak into your life, just so your gift will be unnoticed. He does not want you to utilize what God has given you because he would lose significant recognition. Come on; if you are too blessed to be over stressed, and then your life won't be in a mess. John 10:10 says, The thief cometh not, but to steal, and to kill, and to destroy: I am come that they might have life and that they might have life more abundantly. Many people currently have a life, but are they living more abundantly? Just look around at the many people you know, many are having all kinds of problems. What would make you want to live like them? Though you have a life, is it what you desire? Do you have everything in your life that your heart truly desires? Just think for a moment. If the enemy can have his way in your life, then you will not wish to utilize your gift. Think about it. That is why you must keep your gift in the perfect place, always being prepared. Also, secure your gift around those that are going to encourage you to utilize your gifts. Be with people of the right value, and you too will continue in the right direction. Right now ask yourself these questions, is my gift usable? Am I ready to be used by God, and who or what would I draw in for Him? Can I inspire God? I know when I receive a beautiful gift; I handle it with very special care. My priority is to ensure proper care for the present. Surely, God wants you to take care of your gift(s), show Him how much you value it or them. Would you leave a five karat princess cut diamond sitting out for someone to steal or would you store it away from the thieves? Understand one thing; the enemy has more than just him working; trying to steal from you, he has many workers. You must keep your gifts protected; they are precious. Your gift possesses a life that money can't buy, and it has the potential to destroy the hell out of someone's life – including your own. Now look at that, not just yours but your seeds, the next generation, and vice versa. Your gift is Divine, and it's priceless. Your gift is so potent that it will cause someone's heart to be turned on to Jesus. It is so valuable that it will evict hell out of someone's home, meaning sparing Jesus more hearts, and saving more souls. Your gift also has the authority to make you rich, including all your seeds. Get to know the depth of the power that your gift possesses. It is life threating. Proverbs 10:22 says, The blessings of the Lord, it maketh one rich, and he addeth no sorrow with it.

God wants you to know Him in depth through your heart intentions. Though often our hearts stray from the right intentions we must find our way back. David was one that found himself straying in many ways through many things, but his gifts were specially designed to inspire. Many noticed that his psalms were outstanding; he mightily inspired the hearts of many. David loved his music, and his heart was full of inspirations. Though his battles were great, his victories were even more significant. David had many reasons to inspire God. Sometimes in life things will happen to get us off course, but just remember to get back on. Though the enemy tried to stop David, his mind was set on how powerful his God was. He knew he was being attacked from every angle, but utilizing his gifts kept him protected. 2 Samuel 22:6 says, The sorrows of hell compassed me about; the snares of death prevented me; Understand, David knew that his enemies were great, but he also remembered how the Lord had previously brought him out. During our hell storms, we too must bear in mind our previous victories, our past battles and know that it was only the Lord that has brought us through. A lot of people may not understand what you are going through and no one can tell it as you can. Regardless of what's going on in your life, do not allow the enemy to gain your victory. David was an actual receiver of the word. Remember whatever goes in must come out. David received power every time he received a word from the Lord. As David received a word from the Lord, he also received a moment of inspiration that caused him to satisfy His Lord gladly with utilizing his gifts. Only a receiver of high power can be a true warrior and accomplish great works. 1John 4:4 says, Ye are of God, little children, and have overcome them: because greater is he that is in you, than he that is in the world. You are what you are, and whatever enters is what is going to come out. Psalms 34:1 says, I will bless the Lord at all times; his praise shall continually be in my mouth. David knew there was only one place that he could get fed spiritually, and that was in the presence of The Lord. So many people forsake the assembly of the saints when they are living in sin until it will cause them to lose out on their abundance. I do not know about you, but I want my abundance of life. It is time out for scuffling, half way making it or barely surviving. Jesus came so that we might take part of the wealth. Though the enemy came for another purpose, I am going to live in the abundance – what about you? You have a choice and an opportunity, which one are you going to choose? Are you going to continue to desire to live more abundantly, or are you going to move forward; until you live in the abundance. He wants us to have the best that life has to offer. No, the enemy doesn't want you to want the best because he wants you to be content in life. Why accept his offer, what more could the enemy offer you than Jesus? Figure it out! John 10:10 says, The thief cometh not, but for to steal, and to kill, and to destroy: I am come that they might have life and that they might have it more abundantly. Why just live when you can live more abundantly. Once you begin to live in the abundance, your faith is increased to a level that hell can't stop your praise. That is why the hell has been trying to stop you in your tracks. Hell wants to disconnect you from living more abundantly and to disconnect you from your life promises. The enemy does not wish you to utilize your gifts because God will receive greater glory. Your gift is so valuable; many lives are depending on it and as you utilize them many will be free. People, in general, look at their contributions as just a gift. However, know that your gift will incorporate abundance. IT WILL GIVE ANOTHER AN OPPORTUNITY TO LIVE LIFE MORE ABUNDANTLY. That is why the enemy has tried to stop you from using your gift(s). As I use my gifts, my heart is relaxed in Him. My mind was on Him, and I gain a calmer. Your gift holds the power of life and death; it is valuable. Think about who inspired Billy Graham through a word of encouragement to preach the gospel or who caused him to acknowledge life through the word. What about Martin Luther King, who inspired him through a word of encouragement to become a freedom fighter. There is freedom power in your gift. Do not let the enemy keep your gift suppressed any longer; allow God to receive the glory. Psalms 29:4 says, The voice of the Lord is powerful; the voice of the Lord is full of majesty. David was one that consistently heard from the Lord; it is His voice that will keep you motivated. Allow nothing to keep you away from hearing Him; it is not worth it. I know at one time in my life I needed a word of the Lord as a baby needed milk to survive. I was hungry. My life was being tormented by hell left and right, but I stayed in the word. I felt as though I was being beaten alive; everywhere I turned I received a blow from the enemy; the word gave me new life. No matter what, I never want to grow so big that I can't be a receiver. A receiver is one that's fed, and I want to be as "Spiritually Fed & Spiritually Developed as I can be." The more I'm fed power, the more I can handle the blows of life. That is why it is so valuable to be continually fed the Word so that our gifts can grow. Nothing can destroy the word; it will live forever, and ever. David was always being encouraged by the Word of God because He was a Praiser. Psalms 29:4 says, The voice of the Lord is powerful; the voice of the Lord is full of majesty. Once one that praises hears from The Lord they get excited because they can see God working in their life. Every time God speaks. He merely motivates my heart and excites my praise. When He speaks, my mind is turned from my trouble's and with my blessing. I don't know about you, but I have come too far to turn around now. I have also praised too much for me to think that God doesn't have the power to turn my troubles into a magnificent praise report. It is an actual value to see God speak more so than only to hear Him. Notice, when you see God's WORD, then you will be a force to get up and accomplish because you are going to want what you see. You won't care whose blind to the fact as long as you can see it. If I can see it, then it can exist, and if you can hear Him you can have it. Begin to listen with your eyes. I refuse to give the enemy my praise; nothing interferes with my praise because my abundance is in my praise. 1 Corinthians 2:9 says, But as it is written, Eye hath not seen, nor ear heard, neither have entered into the heart of man, the things which God hath prepared for them that love him. Though I haven't received them yet, I know that it is so. All I need is His word, and His word is enough to motivate my praise. Just as David, though he entered his battles his victory was in his praise.

It doesn't matter who we are or who we are not, we all want to be loved. David utilized his gifts, no matter what. David didn't allow an interference of sin to stop his praise. So many think we can get ourselves together; it is impossible. However, all things are possible through Him. We are all human, we have tendencies to quit, give up, and sometimes we just get tired of trying. No, we still should not quit. My gift tried my patience as it caused me to get more spiritually fit to overcome. It caused my heart to hearken more towards God. It sat me down and caused my heart well as my ears to be attentive towards Him. However, through it all, I was inspired to run. My heart consoled each time I utilized my gifts. They have turned my life completely around and without them, I would be lost.

The enemy does not want you to use your gift that is why He has attacked your faith. He wants you to think it to be impossible. 1 John 4:4 says, Ye are of God, little children, and have overcome them: because greater is he that is in you, than he that is in the world. I looked at myself plenty of times, and I was my worst critic. Often I said, "I cannot write." I gave myself more excuses not to utilize my gifts than I did to utilize them. I bashed myself and always criticized my writings. I want you to know every time we bash our gifts we bash Jesus. I consistently said, "I am nobody and who's going to want my books; I cannot write." Boy, I put myself down more than I exalted God. I did not wish to trust that God had given me the gift of writing. For years, I kept the gift of writing to myself. Admittedly, I shared it with a few family members and friends, but I was not prepared to share it with the world. So every now and again, I began to write. However, one day I realized if I wrote only 15 minutes a day then soon I could finish my first book. At that time, I was writing the book "Aggravated Assault on Your Mind." Then I continued to go through more life struggles. One day God gave me a few figures to add up, and it astonished me. Surely, if I had what He told me to calculate, I would not be suffering financially. Immediately I begin to write more; I grew consistent with writing books. I stopped giving myself excuses because those reasons caused me not to utilize my gift of writing. Every time you down yourself, you show God that you do not appreciate your gift. Today God wants you to receive your gift and then He wants you to adore it. Romans 12:6 says, Having then gifts differing according to the grace that is given to us, whether prophecy, let us prophesy according to the proportion of faith;

Remember faith comes by hearing and not by sight. Once you understand what the Lord is speaking, then your eyes can see it even before you receive it. Instantly in your belly, you will feel the flow of blessings once you receive what the Lord is speaking to you. David was one that received all that God had for him; it didn't matter how large it was – he believed Him for it. His faith was to the extreme, and his praise was potent, David continually inspired God. Have you ever attended a club or a party but, did not join in and have fun.

Well, I know back in the day I didn't, everyone knew that I was in the house. As a believer we need to give God more recognition, after all, we shouted more for the enemy. I refuse to go to a worship service and not worship our Heavenly Father. The key problem today is that most people forget to praise Him to the uttermost while they are in worship. When you are in service, and you feel the Holy Spirit, it will cause a Holy Movement that will begin to anoint the Whole Body of Christ. I do not know what your gifts are, but I know they will bless heaven. Think of the many great spiritual leaders that would have never appreciated their gifts, how many might not have delivered today. Also, the many gifted inspirational singers along with songwriters, perhaps many people would not have received a peace of mind. Whatever your gifts are God wants you to utilize them for His glory. He does not wish you to be ashamed of it, but He wants it to be used. Once you begin to unwrap your gift, you will realize the true value of it. It will reach many hearts and cause many to become more than a conqueror. God has given you something unique, and He wants you to trust His judgments. He chose you and only you; He gave this gift. Ephesians 4; 7 says, But unto every one of us is given an (opportunity to obtain something special from God) grace according to the measure (the full measures) of the gift (perfection of Jesus) of Christ.

David is already known to be more than a conqueror. David held on to God's unchanging hands regardless of what he went through, what he did wrong and what caused his many trials. One that reads is wise, one that seeks shall find and one that asks shall receive. David did it all. He realized that for him just to make it through the next day that he needed to be strengthened. Without power, a man is nothing and David longed for power to overcome. David also knew that His Father was wealthy, meaning God was his every resource.

1John 4:4 says, Ye are of God, little children, and have overcome them: because greater is he that is in you, than he that is in the world. Only God can lead you, guide you and establish you. So, therefore, David took upon him every opportunity that His Father gave him to learn of his gift(s) and to utilize them. Make sure you keep your gift(s) usable for Him because they will follow Jesus.

Chapter Three
Your Presser Releaser

One reason, a gift is so special is because of the happiness it will bring forth. Notice that when you are happy, your day goes better, and your mind feels free. The enemy knows that happiness brings laughter, and that is good. He also knows that it gives our hearts joy. So, therefore, he doesn't want you to get too comfortable in happiness because you would desire it more often. Joy is powerful because then one is entirely free. Allow your gift to bring you happiness, as well as God. David made God happy every time he sang praises, and every time he battled, God was exalted. Your gift can make Him happy too. When you look upon your gift, you will be able to see the blessings that will come from them. Your gift will cause you to live more abundantly through Jesus Christ. Luke 6:21 says, Blessed are ye that hunger now: for ye shall be filled. Blessed are ye that weep now: for ye shall laugh. Though your troubles may be great, and you go through a lot. Afterward, you will know that God is more impressive than any troubled time you endured. Though your tears are flowing, know that your laughter is on its way. I remember when I was truly going through this awful ordeal, boy I was so frustrated and I didn't think I was going to make it, but regardless of how bad things looked I kept my faith. During crucial times in our lives, we get tired of trying. However, just know that your day is coming soon. David was a warrior, and a great one at that because he didn't fear. Often we allow fear to embark on our happiness; we are afraid to move forward. One thing I can say about David is that truly he never needed an army because his faith was perfectly proportioned in God. Ephesians 4; 8 says, Wherefore he saith, "WHEN HE ascended ON HIGH, HE LEAD CAPTIVITY CAPTIVE, AND GAVE GIFTS UNTO MEN".

Another one of David's memorable gifts was winning, he wouldn't settle for less. It did not matter what he had to go against, David wanted his day of joy. He wouldn't let anything stop him from winning. There is complete joy in winning, but we will get back to that in the last chapter. Understand when you win, victory is yours.

Jesus died on the cross for our sins and rose up to all power. As long as you call on Him, nothing can hold you back. Jesus holds the key to release you today from all captivity. God has given you gifts to set you free from bondage. You have to understand that every stronghold over you and every pressure that is within you - He can release from you. Your freedom, your happiness, and your life come through the determination that you have to believe in the power of Jesus. Every day Jesus allows someone through his or her gift(s) to be set free. Once the Spirit of Truth is accepted within your heart, then you shall receive your freedom.

Jesus didn't allow the circumstances that rose up against Him to hold Him down. Withal, He didn't let the people that went against Him to stop Him and neither did David. No matter your battle, know that Jesus is all powerful. David knew him as a Shepherd. Psalms 23:1 says, The Lord is my shepherd I shall not want. And believe me; God took great care of him.

Sometimes we let people control our gift(s) that God has given us. We seek the approval of man and not the attention of God as we need to. For years I was trying to stand up to the standards of man as being a preacher, just wanting them to see that God did call me to minister. I wanted so badly for so many pastors to acknowledge me as a minister of the Gospel. I always thought that being a minister more people would show you greater love. However, the longer I stayed in ministry, the more I realized it is not about them or me. I often said to myself, "If God was for me then who shall be against me." For years, I struggled in the ministry. I struggled with the gift that God had given me, trying to prove to man. One day I finally woke up and said, who cares as long as Jesus cares that is all I need. I wanted Him to care, Him to notice and I decided to please Jesus. God did not give me that particular calling to prove myself to man, but to bring forth glad tidings to the broken and wounded hearts. There are so many people dying daily due to lack of inspirations, and here I was worrying about trying to prove to man, that God called me. I turned that thing around and decided to inspire God so that men can inspire Him too. When someone is down, we should lift them up. We live in a world of many broken spirits. So many people need to be truly inspired. I realized that man did not call me, but my Father which is in Heaven called me to preach the gospel. I had to grow up, mature and develop in Christ. You too must realize that God gave you a special gift, and there is a purpose for every God gave gift. Satisfy Him and watch Him meet you, David knew that too. To you, that mission will seem to be impossible until you find the purpose of your gift. Make God happy by utilizing your gift, to bring Him glory. Philippians 2:2 says, Fulfill ye my joy, that ye be likeminded, having the same love, being of one accord, of one mind. As I continued through the years of ministry, I was developed more in books as I wrote. You will never imagine how far your gift can take you until you become obedient and utilize your gift for Jesus. Allow your gift to bless your life as well as others; it will bring forth greater things. Proverbs 10:22 says, The blessings of the Lord, it maketh rich, and he addeth no sorrow with it.

Often God will already have given you a gift, and you do not even notice it because you have a zillion and one thing on your mind. Understand God cannot present Himself fully until your mind is free and clear. Your mind must be in a position to receive your gift when He presents you with it. Jesus wants you to recognize that He is giving you something greater. John 14:17 says, Even the Spirit of truth; whom the world cannot receive, because it seeth him not, neither knoweth him: but ye know him; for he dwelleth with you, and shall be in you.

You are not an orphan because you are a child of God. Surely, the enemy is trying to tempt you through every stronghold he has over you right now. However, God has not left you alone He is only giving you the backbone to stand on your gift. He is giving you one of the greatest gifts of all, the opportunity to explore – (True Life) His Son Jesus the Christ. The truth is that everyone does not believe and will not receive Jesus because they do not understand Him. No matter how high you search, how low you fall until you receive Jesus in your life, no Gift that God will give you - will be fully developed? Through The Blood of JESUS the Christ, you shall receive strength, might, capability and your spiritual realm will only grow wider, deeper and stronger. When you are developing spiritually, sometimes no matter how much church you are getting, how active you are in the ministry or even your title, we all get to a point where we just need Jesus that much. Jesus knows our weaknesses, and He knows just how much you and I actually can bear.

David was a true warrior; he stood up towards his enemies and won every battle. 2 Samuel Chapter Nine discusses how many victories David had in just one Chapter. Now wonder if David would have feared to go against his enemies, he would have still been pressured? When you want your pressures of life released, you will fight to win. You will stand in faith and utilize what God has given you to the fullest. Now, what if David would have thought he wasn't strong enough to fight against the Philistines, or what If he would have aborted himself in battle? Now if you read this chapter, after each battle David was richly blessed with each victory. He would have also aborted his many blessings. David kept in mind how awesome his God was, and he knew Him as a shield. So, therefore, David was always protected by the Greatest Life Protector. Psalms 3:3 says, But thou, O Lord, art a shield for me; my glory, and the lifter up of mine head. Even when you are going through, He will lift you up. That gift that you have is your pressure releaser. It doesn't matter what you are going through, just know that you are an overcomer. Now allow your gift to take you to your next level, gain your next victory until you triumph in life. Use your gift to satisfy Jesus and believe me; He will surely make your laughter generate your happiness.

Chapter Four
Can God Is Depend On Your Gift?

God wants to pull you away from the usual crowd that is why He did not give you a common gift. Jesus does extraordinary works by calling you out of an average crowd. Matthew 20:16 says, So the last shall be first, and the first last; for many be called, but few chosen. He called you because you possess an extraordinary quality, which is why He has given you this gift. It will bring Him Extraordinary Glory. Can you imagine being that One that will cause God to receive Extraordinary Glory? David did, and he was forever blessed. He wants to anoint you so that this work assignment that He has given you will be a Divine Work. Allow the Anointing to Surface as you exercise your gift(s). The assignment that God has given you through your gift is a secular work. It is for The GREAT I AM to be magnified in a work that He expects of you. This gift is yours; it was assigned just for you to utilize it. God expects great things from you, which is why He has called you out of a usual crowd. When God appointed you, He looked at your qualifications; He checked your background. He allowed you to pass numerous tests. Your test has qualified you for this work. You met all of His qualifications; now He requires something more powerful for you. God no longer wants you to be just an ordinary person. He wants you to be that peculiar vessel - the one that can and will get the job done. You have "Can Do Power" in your gift, every time you think you can't just say it aloud, "I Can Do This." Deuteronomy 14:2 says, For thou art a holy people unto the LORD thy God, and the LORD hath chosen thee to be a peculiar people unto himself, above all the nations that are upon the earth. He has thought mighty highly of you to accept even you for this work; now He wants you to think higher of yourself. He wants this job assignment that He has given you to be complete. I have told many people through my years in ministry that if you don't believe in yourself, then no one else will. If you want to achieve greater, then reach higher. Additionally, if you want something done right, you must do it yourself. However, this one person told me, "I can show you better than I can say – just watch my feet." He wants you to be stronger and full of The Anointing Performance from the work of your hands. It is your production time to prove to yourself that God has assigned you this job. You will most definitely know that this vision was from God once you finish it. He wants your gift to survive, faith without works are dead. God is a faithful God, and every word that proceeds out of His mouth will bring forth a production of truth, it will be fully developed because He spoke it. Once The Holy Spirit speaks, then it is so! Jesus has mastered Life to the fullness, and He has the Power to Raise the Dead. Exercise your gift. Matthew 8:22 says, But Jesus said unto him, Follow me; and let the dead bury the dead.

Let your gift live. Keeping your gift buried is like burying life alive. Someone needs to see your gift come to live because someone depends on your present to survive. There is hope for your gift and joy for another's heart with love that will caress a soul. You will be amazed at how a good song will inspire someone. Your gift is needed, and someone needs it more than you. Allow the Anointing to surface through utilizing your present. For years, I allowed my tips to stay buried, because of lack of exercising my gifts. Perhaps, the gift that God has given you will help many in their time of need. Now look upon that gift and ask yourself, is it worth living? And if so, begin to utilize it and let God birth that baby out of you. Just as God assigned Noah to build the Ark, He did not ask Noah's son, nor his wife or any other friend or family member. God had this assignment set-aside especially for

Noah, not Moses, not Jeremiah nor Mary, but Noah. He knew that only Noah could build an ark that met all of His specifications. There was only one that God could depend on to build the ark, and it could only be Noah. Perhaps if God had called on Moses, he probably would have gotten tired too soon. Jeremiah may have been shouting too much, and he too could not have finished the work. Mary would not have had the arm strength and the building techniques to handle such a workload. God knew that she was a virgin to birth baby Jesus. Work that God has chosen for you is just for you. Luke 7:14 says, And he came and touched the bier: and they that bare him stood still. And he said, Young man, I say unto thee, Arise. Whatever it is that God is expecting you to do, it cannot happen until you decide to finish your work. God chose Moses to lead many out of bondage, but He only allowed Noah to lead 8, including himself, by building the ark. God knew just how much Moses could bear and how much Noah could bear. Remember as you work this vision with your hands, God won't put more on you than you can bear. However, to many, the eight being led to safety looked like nothing compared to the amount of people that Moses lead out of captivity. Well, if it had not been for the eight that Noah led out, then this world would not even be in existence today. Noah built the ark for eight people, including all the animals that he led out as he followed precise instructions from God, which is the reason you and I are here today. Now, what if Noah would have just led the eight out, but forgot the animals or built a boat instead an ark. God intended him to build an ark because a boat would not have been able to hold all of them, or survive the rainstorm. I believe that nowadays we want to do many things our way after we have received our gifts from God. We sometimes want the easy way out, but with God, there is no easy way out. God is a God of firm instructions, and every instruction is for a Divine Purpose. Just as David stood to battle with the Philistines, it wasn't easy – but he fought until he won. When he went to Moab, it wasn't easy – but David fought until he gained the victory. No battle is easy; the victory is always rewarding. Fight until you win. However, what and who were saved through Noah's obedience was just enough to anticipate God to create again. As we want God, He begins to please us more. He will make things that have died in your life come to life again, such as dreams and visions. He will also make what has been washed away, come back greater in our life. I tell you we serve an awesome God. As we listen to Him, He will give us the same precise instructions to release the fullness of our gifts. God has a plan for your gift to produce more life. Through your determined effort, God is going to make someone else stand firmer, get motivated and most of all become usable for him. Now notice that Noah did not focus on all the materials he needed or the equipment to build such an ark. Many things were not available at His hands to reach. However, God brought the things as he needed them. God gave Noah every piece of wood, every nail and everything else from the ground up, even giving him a ladder of hope as he built the ark. Today God wants your faith all the way, to the top of your vision. Take your mind off the needed things to make this work gain life. However, put your thoughts on the Powerful God that can touch any dead thing and give it new life. Talk about all the needed materials Noah did not have, but he built the ark compared to today's materials. David also knew Him as his Rock. Psalms 18:2 says, The Lord is my rock, and my fortress, and my deliverer; my God, my strength, in whom I will trust; my buckler, and my horn of my salvation, and my high tower.

Just as the widow walking with the crowd on her way to bury her only child, Jesus was in her by passing, but He did not pass her by. St. Luke 7 verses 11 through 15. Jesus saw and felt her heart. Though her son was dead, lying in a coffin on the way to his burial ground, Jesus looked at the coffin and spoke to her son and said, "Young man, I say unto thee, Arise. So the boy arose, and he begins to speak." He walked his way out of death. That young man walked out of a dead man's coffin on the way to his burial ground. When the Lord speaks, it is so. No matter what you are going through, know that The Lord is speaking and weep not. Today Jesus says speak life. Speak it so, until that dead gift comes to life. Proverbs 15:4 says, A wholesome tongue is a tree of life: but a perverseness therein is a breach in the spirit. Allow the stronghold of the enemy that is binding down your vision hear what thus said the Lord. Speak to your gift and watch the death hold be removed in the name of Jesus. The power right now is on your tongue. Speak with power, use that power of Anointing and speak unto your vision. In the name of Jesus tell your gift to get up. Watch how the movement begins to take place in your life. As that young man heard the voice of Jesus, he gained life because of The Anointing Power that was in the voice of the Lord. Sometimes if you cannot feel that anointing in your gift, then you must speak it into existence. If Jesus did, then so can you. However, you choose to use the Anointing Powers of God, just use them. Right now claim your victory for your vision. Speak to your gift in the name of Jesus; declare this work to be done. Matthew 12:34 says, O Ye generations of vipers, how can ye being evil speak good things? For out of the abundance of the heart the mouth speaketh.

Your mind will be made up, and you will be prepared to move forward. Know that the power that is in JESUS' name is considered to be The Accomplisher. There is nothing that He hasn't accomplished and anything you need Him to accomplish, and He will. He gives us the strength to excel in life when we want to. It is time to make some needed changes in your life, to explore the true revelation of this gift that God has given you. Don't you want it to come to pass, if so then make some changes? These changes can only happen through the power that is in the name of JESUS. Also, you must prepare yourself to do some things that you normally wouldn't do. You can do it, just tell yourself every time you think you can't - that you can. There are expectations from God for you to finish, it is a work that has been specially formulated for every cell that God has formed within your body. This gift was specially created and made just for you. Every blood vessel, every bone structure, every fingertip; God designed this for you. The structure of the cells is especially designed for you to do it. There is no way around it because once you begin, it will be complete. Just as God has given you this gift, He also has your reward. Surely, you want to receive the full benefit of your reward once God fulfills this gift. Philippians 2:2 says, Fulfill ye my joy that ye be like-minded, having the same love, being of one accord, of one mind; of mighty works that will fill you with joy and that will allow a multitude also to rejoice in it after the finishing of it. Though this work is not complete yet, God said, "Work it," "Finish it," and "Let it Surface" because He has spoken it. Understand one thing that this is the most valuable thing, when God gives an assignment it will go forth. Oh, it's all going to happen, but you may not be the receiver of the reward unless you finish it. If you are obedient to the call of this work that God has given you, then you will receive an incredible reward. Look at your hands one more time, notice its appearance and think of what could all come from it when you finish. God has certain duties that must be performed by certain servants. I have never known of a servant of the Lord that did not gain The Anointing or served Him powerlessly. These powers are designated only for the ones that The Lord appoints for the services that He need or want for a True Divine Purpose. There is absolutely no way to hide from the service call that God has given His appointed servers to do. God has given you a Special Divine Assignment that will lead, guide and be a light of truth for many to follow. He has a plan just for the gift He has given you. Your gift was designed to deliver. Believe me; God has a plan that will never fail. By now surely, your vision has been made clear to you. Just note the facts, when God gives you a duty serve well. Be the best that you can, because you have been called to duty by The Creator! Many people look upon a calling as becoming a preacher no that is not true. God has called many to duty, but they never cared to receive true instructions. Surely, God has called many to preach and teach but maybe not to lead. Today many run, and open up a church when that is not what God has called them to do. Sometimes we hear only part of the instruction; some can get so excited until they run before God finishes giving the instructions. God gives us instructions to follow as He calls us to become His servants. We all have a calling; God calls all of us to do some form of good service for Him, but many refuse to listen as He speaks. However, all appeals are not called to preach nor teach the gospel. Some callings are for some form of charity. It could also be to start a new business that will offer more job opportunities. Moreover, some are just called to preach and teach the word. However, all callings will be a form of help, inspiration, encouragement and that will build up lives through one-way or another. All visions are not just in the church; many are on the outside. Our duty is to create, inspire and to bring forth light in the world - through the many operable gifts of God. Be prepared to be used for the glory of God and continue to exercise your gifts.

Chapter Five
Properly Insure Your Gift (s)

The Anointing is an appointment to gain power which can only flow from heaven. Once the anointing comes upon you, then you are His. Often many try to run, but they simply can't hide from God. Your life will not be right until you obey Him. David was one that was insured by God that he was completely covered. Do you realize every time you win a battle, it's another testimony? Every time you overcome one thing, it is your strength that helps you to endure another. And every time David exercised his gifts for the Lord, God increased his coverage. David continued to try to please God, and God continued to look after David. As God anoints you, then you will be immediately set completely apart from the rest, and you will become a peculiar person. You will have gone through something in your life that you know only God had brought you through. Nobody can anyone testify to it as you can. Surely, in your life, there will be some very life noticeable changes. Exodus 19:5 says, Now, therefore, if ye will obey my voice indeed, and keep my covenant, then ye shall be a peculiar treasure unto me above all people; for all the earth is mine.

The things you used to do will no longer be of interest to you. Some people you used to hang with, you won't be able to withstand their company anymore. If God is for you, then who cares who is against you. Your life's intention will be finally focused on pleasing God because now you will know the full consequences of not pleasing Him. Your day's journey will begin in praise from the heart for God, all because you can't forget just how far He has brought you. And can't you feel that Anointing brewing in your gifts. Can you feel that unspeakable joy is flowing all through your heart? Our Heavenly Father is worth praising? I have heard this over and over; I want to shout but I can't.

Baby, when I just look back over my life – I shout. It doesn't take me to look back too far; the Lord has blessed me so much. I have been through the wringer, if only you knew that just one breath is worth a praise. To have my family living under the same roof is praise. For me to utilize my right side after my stroke, is worth a praise. I have more than enough reasons to praise Him. I can imagine why David loved to honor, his war times were great, and his battles were even more significant. The Lord allowed him not only to survive but to be a winner. David had to prove constantly that he served a Mighty and Awesome God. Through Every battle, every war and every victory David proved how awesome God is. Psalm 55:16 says, As for me, I will call upon God; and the Lord shall save me.

It is so wonderful that He has thought enough of you; I consider it a life set up. Remember all the times you felt so down that you couldn't get up, wasn't it God that set you up. All those times that you thought you were not going ever to be worth anything. Look at how God thought more of you than you thought of yourself. That downfall you went through was just for God to anoint the works of your hands. Perhaps, if things in your life had never happened like they did, then God would have never been able to give you this vision. Thank Him for every downfall because only He has set you up. God wants you to receive His promises and obey what He tells you because He has some treasures waiting for you that money just can't buy. Psalm 25:14 says, The secret of the Lord is with them that fear him, and he will show them his covenant. David was covered because He knew how to inspire God. He satisfied God with his praise as he continuously gave God his undivided attention. David believed in giving God His time. Truly when he worshiped, it was God's time. David didn't let anything or anyone interrupt his day to share with God. His praise was his proof that The Almighty was his life protector. He caressed God's heart every time he appreciated and utilized his gifts. He proved to God, just how much he understood Him.

This Power is not a Power of man or self-flesh, but it is a Power of Affliction that is forever lasting. You cannot run from the Anointing Powers of God no matter how hard you try. It will cause your heart to agree with the Spirit of God. You will do things that you never thought you would be able to do. You will be able to touch people, and they will be instantly healed. As you speak, The Spirit of God will be your life speaker. As you open your mouth, even the dead shall hear. Whatsoever you begin to talk, it all shall come to pass. Your hands will do works that it never dreamed. Your eyes will see larger, and your goals will expand until it causes you to make a move. Your visions will grow within your Spirit that will cause a multitude to be saved. 1 John 2:27 says, But the anointing which ye have received of him abideth in you, and ye need not that any man teach you: but as the same anointing teacheth you all things, and is truth, and is no lie, and even as it taught you, ye shall abide in him.

You will not even have to open your mouth for the WORDS of God to speak. As you walk you will be a lighthouse for the lost. You will also be a doctor in the sick room alone just by being present. The enemy will fear you as you walk; he will flee out of your way as he feels your presence drawing nearer. In addition, to sum it all up, you will simply scare hell to death. You will destroy the tricks of the enemy. You will steal the life out of hell as you will begin to bruise the enemy. Psalm 23:5 says, Thou preparest a table before me in the presence of mine enemies: thou anointest my head with oil; my cup runneth over. You will kill the lies out of every deceitful life that you are around. The anointing is contagious; it will cause others that are in your presence to connect with RIGHTEOUSNESS. It is like an air born disease, it will touch anyone that gets in its way just to let them know that it is contagious and All – Powerful. It is The Yoke Destroyer. Truly many people do not understand the Anointing, they think because they shout from time to time that they have felt the Anointing. On the other hand, if they get a little too emotional some time they have experienced the Anointing. If they cry in service and cannot stop, they thought they felt the Anointing. Well I am here to tell you, that's not the Anointing. The Anointing comes once The Hands of the Lord is Upon You. The Anointing is the yoke destroyer and there will be a true change that will take place in your life. I am speaking of behind the closed door changes that only you know the Lord knows about. This change will begin secretly just between you and the Lord. Just because you have felt feverless hot at times, that wasn't the anointing. Though fire had run through your inner soul, or you fell out in the midst of a worship service, well that isn't the Anointing either. Once the Anointing comes upon you, it will put a Spirit of Righteousness deep inside you. You will simply desire to do what is right, there is no compromise. The Anointing will grow at large until it consumes the flesh up out of you. The Anointing will destroy the yokes inside of you, fry it up, and flip it over until all the yokes are gone. It is time for you to claim your acceptable year of the Lord. God is getting ready to give it all to you, through the life of your work. Life more abundantly, life over flowing and life posing all power. Are you ready for this New Life Production? Psalm 34:1 says, I will bless the Lord at all times: his praise shall continually be in my mouth. David had numerous reasons to praise, and he knew his praise was only for God. No one ever had to persuade him to go and serve God, he knew whom he served. David's heart was always in preparation to praise. He didn't allow his troubles, problems, battles or even sin stop His praise. You will be amazed how powerful God praise can be, it will cause the flood gates of heaven to pour out abundance for you. It will consume your enemies and cause your battles to be won. It will give you heavenly power, meaning the doors in your life will begin to open that no man will ever have the authority to shut. That is why David was so blessed, because he constantly praised God. He knew that he simply owed God His praise. The greater your praise is the more significant your victory. David's praise report was so long, sometimes he couldn't tell it all, so therefore he had to dance out the rest. When you realize the hell that God has removed out of your life, no one will ever have to persuade you to praise Him. It will utter itself out of you. When you realize how powerful your God is, then a worry will not be on your mind, but your victory praise will. David loved to worship God; he knew his God deserved praise every time he just thought of his goodness.

Hasn't God been a wonderful God to you, awesome I know. Just remember to give Him His praise; those are His praises and not yours. He is worthy and at all times, I do owe Him praise. Just as you desire your blessings, He desires His praise – it's His glory. So excuse me, if you see me in a grocery store, giving Him His praise. Just ignore me if you see me at a stop light giving Him His praise. I most definitely owe Him my life, because of the hell alone that He has brought me through. I'm going to give Him His praise. Those are His praises, not mine. No one can do me like He has, what about you? I once ran into this Apostle that thought I was a babe in Christ, surely I am. One thing about a child is that they are always prepared to listen to their guardians. A child will be obedient and they know the consequences of dis-obedience. David was one that continued in his child-like faith. He never grew too large for God, or too high that he couldn't praise Him. I have also felt like David. No one knows the troubles I have been through, and no one could praise Him like I can. The many storms that He has carried me through, believe me I owe Him my praise. When everyone turned their back on me, He was there. He has truly been my high tower, I owe Him praise. Often times many will begin to gain so much; until now they will feel as though they are too grown too praise. Well, David always allowed his heart to stay as a child's heart towards Go; that is why his praise greatly satisfied heaven. A child is always excited to see their daddy and David was always excited to glorify his Heavenly Father. Allow recognition to be continually in your mouth, uplift and inspire God; after all, He rightfully deserves to always be praised.

Chapter Six
Maintain Your Coverage

You must know who you are to the Lord, David knew who he was. He was the chief musician, one that was skillful and great. He was also a warrior with many recorded defeats. He was a worshipper that loved to dance. On the other hand, he also had a lot of spiritual distractions that tried to hinder his progress. His heart poured out as he arranged the worship services of the temple. Yes, he was a worship instructor too. And I wondered for many of years, why was he so blessed despite all of his sins. One thing I realized about God, He doesn't put his focus on our sins, but He notices our inner being. God knows exactly who we are through our heart's intentions. 1 Chronicles 6:31 says, And these are they whom David set over the service of song in the house of the LORD, after that the ark had rest. No matter who you are, we all need to maintain our coverage in the LORD. Sin is so easy to entangle in, most of the time you will commit it and then realize it later. Sin is strong and its purpose is to stop us from worshiping our Lord. David wasn't a fool, he knew that too. Sin has powers that only you yourself can give, don't feed it to your soul. No one can overcome sin. Without The Lord – No One! Sin only wants to feed your mind the many reasons not to serve the Lord, so that perhaps it can stop your worship. Worship is all powerful; it will release every strong enemy and cause them to flee out of your life. Now think of how once your enemies are out of your way, nothing will hinder you from excelling in life. The enemy doesn't want to see you progress. Most assuredly, once you excel in life your praise will excel too. In addition, your worship will excel and God's Glory will be exalted - more through you. The full purpose of sin is to control your praise – the enemy wants to STEAL, KILL & DESTROY your Worship and Praise from the LORD. Hasn't he taken enough from you? He isn't worth one more thing, not even your praise and worship. Give God His Praise and ADORATION and, watch how He will remove all of your enemies. Understand in our life time we all must endure some things that are going to break us down or either identify who we are. Every battle I had to fight was a battle that trained me for more, encouraged me for greater, and a test that I had passed. When life punches come at you, the majority of times they are unexpected. Yes, it hurts but you must fight back. David was able to stand against so much, because he knew how to inspire God. He was a true worshiper and his worship kept him covered. No matter what rose up against David or perhaps what kind of sin he had encountered, he adored utilizing his gifts to satisfy God. No one had to convince David that he was one of the greatest warriors, greatest faith walkers, and greatest psalmist. David knew that he was nothing without his LORD, he knew his Savior.

Don't let anyone tell you any different. I once knew this person and he tried to persuade me of some things about why we shouldn't go to church. I too had been hurt in the church, but he didn't understand all that the LORD has brought me through. This conversation we had wasn't an explanation to me, because I knew JESUS. As I told him of my troubles, I called on the name of JESUS, and He heard my cry. When my children were deeply in need, I called on the name of JESUS, and He was my way maker. When people spitefully criticized and used me I called on the name of JESUS, He was there. No other has blessed me as He has. No matter what I have done in my life, no other has forgiven me as He has and no one can love me as He can. All my life I called on His name, and He has continuously saved me. Regardless of what man is trying or thinking that they are doing to the house of God, I'm going to give God His praise. There is nothing like the power of The Most High and He is sweet I know.

David was the one that arranged worship for the house of the LORD. He was the minister of music, able to excite the hearts of the congregation. He caused hearts to praise as they worshiped. He was the one that introduced the congregation to worship as he ministered in song. Can you imagine, being the one that will cause people to notice God let alone worship HIM. Well, David soothed the hearts of many as he caused them to worship His Heavenly Father. 1 Chronicles 6:32 says, And these are they whom David set over the service of song in the house of the LORD, after that the ark had rest. He had a purpose to introduce them to His Heavenly Father, David knew of spiritual distractions. He knew how hard it was just to enter into the gates of His Heavenly Father. David heavily encountered many problems. He was being spiritually tormented in many ways. The enemy wanted to stop David from ever receiving all that God had promised him. The enemy tried everything he could to get David to not go forth. That is why his battles were so great; the enemy was hoping that during one of his war times that someone would kill him. If you noticed, David, even as a child being the one that destroyed a powerful Giant, it caused others to question their faith. As many looked upon David, they saw true victories of his God. Truly He caused many to marvel as they probably said, "How did he do that?" Well God wants the same effect from your life. He wants to take the giants in your life out, but you must maintain your coverage. Notice, David was being empowered every time he was able to minister in music. David was being fed every time he was being preached to. David also was being encouraged, just alone by entering the gates. In addition, he was completely rejuvenated to be prepared for what was to come; he gained new strength. There is so much when you enter into The Presence of The LORD. I don't know about you, but there is nothing like taking a moment out of your busy day, just to adore your God. David knew Him as his all in all. He rescued David more times than any other recorded in the bible. He blessed David through the greatest battles and still until this day more Bible readers always can find a word in the book of Psalms. Despite all of David's spiritual distractions, he still took the time to praise and worship God. I can only testify to what I know, living life trying to overcome is extremely challenging, and I can't do it by myself. What about you? As we go through life's strongholds, we must maintain our coverage. It is a time that we must truly prove our faith, we must stand. When that day comes in your life, and you are pushed into a brick wall, you can't step backwards. You must be determined to move forward, despite that wall, and any other spiritual distractions. You can only depend on supernatural strength with an expectancy to be moved. David did, and he was moved each time. You will just simply need a Miracle Worker. David did and God worked many just for him. Often times we get into those kinds of situations, but in the midst we need to maintain our coverage. David assembled all the time in the house of The LORD, utilizing his gift of God kept him covered. I'm not perfect, but every time I call on Him, He is always there. We all fall short of His Glory sometimes - we all need to be inspired, uplifted, motivated and encouraged to run on. The house of the LORD is where you can stay covered. I once heard this Apostle say, keep your problems out of the house of the LORD! I wondered who this Apostle was serving. Understand that the house of the LORD is a "Spiritual Hospital," it's a place for Spiritual Healing, Spiritual Deliverance and Spiritual Motivation. So that is why I believe David stayed covered. He knew the house of the LORD was his Spiritual Hospital. He was

Spiritually Sick and he needed to be Spiritually Delivered. He was Spiritually Wounded and he needed to be Spiritually Healed. He was Spiritually Broken and he needed to be Spiritually Mended. Gathering with the saints may not look like that much to you, but it was everything to David and he stayed covered. Every time he utilized his gifts, he encourages someone else and their inspirations caused him to stay Spiritually Motivated! When you enter into sin, it is a spiritual distraction. There is only one way to defeat it and that is with supernatural courage to continue to resist it. Overcoming life's obstacles and sin is a spiritual warfare. David had to allow the presence of The Lord to minister to him; that is why praise continuously came out of his mouth. He knew that he wasn't perfect, he was a sinner and he didn't try to hide it. Psalms 37:4 says, Delight thyself also in the LORD; and he shall give thee the desires of thine heart.

If David could hold on to nothing else, he held on to this word. If I delight myself in God, He will give me the desires of my heart. David continuously tried to prove to God that he was delighting himself in Him. Everything David needed, only God had the power to produce. Man couldn't possibly possess David's future; he desired things that money couldn't purchase. David desired a title that required more than what he currently had. He needed conquering power, great integrity, substantial stability and all that would fit with a title of becoming a KING. His heart's desire was greater than what he had, so therefore God had to allow his challenges to bring forth many great victories. David's entire test was to prepare him for the life, the power and wealthy lifestyle of becoming a King. So therefore, your heart's desires will sometimes cause your life challenges to be more than you can bear just too spiritually equip you with what you truly will need to succeed.

David desired some great things of the LORD, just think of all he had to endure. Just as you must endure, you too must desire to come out. Sometimes, your coming out is harder than your going through period and the strength alone that you will need is powerful. Well, David was a great warrior, and he needed power to overcome, strength to battle and will power to succeed. Just imagine war after war, battle after battle, and victory each time. Yes, David was extremely wealthy in faith as he continuously proved to God that He was his LORD. How many times have you quit proving to God, utilizing your gifts or making excuses all because of someone or something. It is not worth it. God can't receive any glory out of that. There have been many times I too was angry and didn't want to go to church because of something or someone; perhaps, there were things I needed to do, but I didn't because of something or someone. Truly, I was only hindering my progress. I no longer wanted my blessings aborted. Often we are so close to our next breakthrough; we can touch it. However, we quit and give up too soon. Our excuses are not worth it; we only abort our prosperity.

Do you remember hearing from the LORD at all? A lot of times I listened to the Holy Spirit speak to me with innovations in a form of success, and His word was so fulfilling. It has caused me to expect these things to come to pass, what about you? I decided not to give up that easily just because my life looked like it was in a rumble. No, I decided to fight for what I believed in. The Lord has spoken too many wonderful things in my hearing, if you only knew the half of what I had to endure. Life can be extremely challenging at times, it can make you question yourself as well as prove your faith. Though hell has occasionally risen up in my life, I had to allow my faith to exceed to the next level - anyhow. Listen, God is speaking to you. David was one that heard his voice, even with his spiritual distractions. 11 Samuel 22:20 says, He brought me forth also into a large place: he delivered me, because he delighted in me. David knew Him as a DELIVERER; know Him as your DELIVERER. He will bring you out into a place to call your own. No one will be able to claim your land, your territory and not even your blessings. As God blessed David, everyone was able to see and say that The Lord's Hands were upon him. Continue to use what the LORD has given you, and excel in life. Stop allowing people, things, circumstances and situations to cause spiritual distractions to stop you. If you have too many spiritual distractions where you are, then relocate because your future is depending on it. Every distraction in your life is a hindrance, and sometimes you must go. David knew the LORD had delivered him from his strong enemy, he wasn't expecting to be held back any longer. Just as he eventually became King, you too will eventually succeed just as long as you maintain your coverage. Allow God to receive His glory and watch how He will keep you covered. Regardless of your circumstances, situations, battles and spiritual distractions, He got you covered. The battle is not yours, it is the Lord's - so what are you worried about? 11 Samuel 22:30 says, For by thee I have run through a troop: by my God have I leaped over a wall. Allow God to cause you to leap over walls, to run with the victory, and see what your end is going to be. All that he did for David, He can do it for you too. Maintain your coverage because your future depends on it.

Chapter Seven
Your Destiny Is Packed In Your Gift

The key to unlocking your destiny is useful pushing purpose? I have claimed some beautiful and expensive things in my lifetime. More than an average income could supply. Only my faith could deliver me, so, therefore, I realized I had to utilize my gifts. Your destiny is in your purpose, and your heart will lead you to your destiny. If, you follow your heart.

Psalm 84:11 says, For the Lord God is a sun and shield: the Lord will give grace and glory: no good thing will he withhold from them that walk uprightly. Keep your promises in your sight, never letting them go. The Lord rewards those that deserve it. Know that you are doing something that deserves awards, and then expect your prize. Occasionally, go by and put claims on things that you can't afford, but that your heart desires. Touch some things that are tasteful and useful, want them with a passion. Post them in your eyesight. Just stay reminded of everything that God said He was going to do for you. God spoke to me when I was going through, and I could not see my way out. My eyes saw darkness, but my heart felt the light. My bank account was negative, but God told me I was rich. I claimed things that my money could not buy in a 10-year life span, but God told me you are going to be able to pay cash for it. He is a God of His word and His word is true. Make sure you keep your purpose in your eyesight. It is just like a child wanting candy, and as long as they can crave the sweetness, they will do what you tell them to do to get it. Post it up on your mirror, in your kitchen, office or perhaps on your car dashboard- just keep it in your sight. As long as you can keep your eyes on the prize, then you will run and not get tired. You will recognize the power that is in your gift(s). Your faith will grow because you will be able to keep your hope alive. Keep your visions in your sight, hold on to them. Post it where you can see it every day. Allow your goals to be seen by your eyes and think of your result. Stand on it and don't be moved, no matter how hard times get; just hold on to your prize as if you have already won it. When you hold onto it in that manner, then you will finish what you have started. If you hold onto it as if you already have it, then you are walking through the finish line with your arms up. God Is Waiting On You At The Finish Line. Ecclesiastes 9:11 says, I returned, and saw under the sun, that the race is not to the swift, nor the battle to the strong, neither yet bread to the wise, nor yet riches to men of understanding, nor yet favor to men of skill, but time and chance happened to them all. God wants you to know that He is waiting for you at the finish line, and He wants His praise even before you complete this task. It's your chance to get it right, so, that He can bless you righteously. He is trying to give you – your heart's desires. He has your new life waiting at the finish line. He is rooting for you to run on. Your hope for tomorrow is in every forward step that you make right now. The harder you run, the more hope you'll gain. Your joy unspeakable is at the finish line of this journey. If you could ask Isaiah, Job, and Abraham how did they make it – surely they will tell you it wasn't easy. God is sure that they will tell you to keep moving forward, hold onto your faith, and through it all just trust God. They kept stepping forth, and they did not let anything stop them. Though times they may have tarried, and times they may have come to a halt, but they never stopped taking their steps forward. Though sin sometimes may have gotten them off the right track, it was the love of God that routed them to their finish line. Though the road was hard, and sometimes they got discouraging, they kept on moving anyhow. They kept their eyes prepared and ready to see the finish line of faith. Your prosperity is at the finish line, your wealth, and all your promises are waiting for you at the finish line. All those things that you have ever imagined good to happen in your life are at the end of your finish line - along with every heart drenching prayer. By the way, the more laps you run the sooner you will get to the finish line. The more effort you put in the works of your hands, the sooner you will be rewarded. Regardless of your skills, God can use them for His glory. He wants you to take what you have, and run with it. No matter how fit you are for this journey; continue to allow Gods Anointing Power to get you in perfect shape. That idea, and dream; that gift is all yours because God gave it to you. Now, move with it, step in it and live it to the fullness, because God's Anointing Power is in it. He wants your hands on it so that you can live your acceptable year of the Lord.

Isaiah 61:2 says, To proclaim the acceptable year of the Lord, and vengeance of our God; to comfort all that mourn. Now God is transforming all of your nothings into something. He is bringing forth the evidence that He has heard your cry. All those long nights that you yielded your heart unto Him, you poured out from your belly the hell that has tormented you. Also, all those enemies that stole your possessions took the things you love for a selfish gain. They tried to destroy you. Romans 12:14 says, Bless them which persecute you: bless and not curse. As He visits your enemies, He will let them know who you are in Him. He will cause them to have to come unto you with blessings and good deeds seeking forgiveness. God will restore everything that was taken out of your life, as He restores you. You will be more blessed with bigger, and better. It is your Hallelujah time because the victory is now yours. All that mourned when you mourned, prayed, and cried along by your side will receive the overflow of your blessings. They too will be restored. Oh, now He is straightening out some crooked stuff within your enemies that caused you to cry, and that upset you. It is just as a child that got beat up by that neighborhood bully, and ran home to tell their daddy, boy a daddy wouldn't let anyone beat up their child, and get away with it. That daddy is going to be like a wolf. He's going to straighten out the bully, and as they see the dad coming down the street, they are going to know that trouble is on its way. Immediately, they will begin to fear. So don't worry about your enemies. God will have all vengeance against every enemy that has ever come up against you. Because when they come to you, they messed around with a child of God. That is why Satan is sitting in hell right now because He messed around with God. The enemy forgot that Jesus has the keys to hell, and guess what, He is your vindicator. Just as long as you are in God, and He is in you, and then you too possess those same keys to hell. I mean every part of it, so do not worry. Romans 12:19 says, Dearly beloved, avenge not yourselves, but rather give place unto wrath: for it is written, vengeance is mine; I will repay, saith the Lord.

Just keep in mind that God did it all for you. He remembered every heavy load, every burden that you carried and every weight that you lifted while you were trying all that you had. Just because many hurt you as you tried, God does not ever want you to turn out to be another one of them. He wants you always to walk in love, kindness, and to do many good deeds as a righteous warrior that has won the battle. God is going to turn your entire life around. The work of your hands is going to prove to many that the Hands of The Lord Is upon You. It will be noticeable to all to see that God is in you. So, therefore, continue to represent in Love. Represent in a right manner, be a real God ambassador. Romans 12:21 says, Be not overcome by evil, but overcome evil with good.

For every time that you were confused, and you brought to shame, God is going to grant you a double to a hundred-fold return. Your reward will be your inheritance; it calculated for your portion of faith. If you grow large in faith, then your part will be great. If you only have a little faith, then your inheritance part will be small. However, if your faith has no limits on how much God can bless you, then your legacy will never stop calculating. Once you finish here on this earth, absolutely no one will be able to count your value. Remember what He had told you. Well, now it is at an all-time high; just as if the stock market has hit the top of the roof and your increase breaks through. God is going to grant you more than you can imagine for all your troubles. Your acceptable year (BIG YEAR) is the year that God will find, and bestow the favor of increase upon you. Every stronghold that binds you; through every locked down and imprisoned situation, God said, "It's your FREEDOM TIME."

Heaven is about to release every promise that God promised you, just because you held out, and held on. God is unlocking every locked up blessing that kept you from prospering. You know all those dreams that you have had, and God brought forth a new covenant, well it is pay-day time, payback time, and over-pay time. Your gain is going to be larger than your eyes could ever see. Why, because you trusted the Lord to be your help. When everyone belittled you, laughed at you, and scandalized you – you held on. Why, because you have been crazy enough to believe in all these crazy dreams that God was going to do this thing for you. So, therefore, God is going to give you every desire of your heart; including the desires that you have forgotten. Isaiah 61:8 says, For I the LORD love judgment, I hate robbery for burnt offering; and I will direct their work in truth, and I will make an everlasting covenant with them.

Now you know that God has anointed your hands for this job because it is now fruitful, and multiplying if it has not yet then it will. Only God can cause such an enrichment of prosperity, and joy to come into your life. God loves satisfying with the truth that is why the truth shall set you free. As one of my good friend's mother always says, "Baby one thing God loves, it isn't anything but the truth, and I tell you that's what He loves." His Anointing Powers has the key that is going to cause those closed doors to open as you begin to walk towards them. When the tree of David had been cut down, the stump still had life in it. Though many things seemed to try to cut down the works of your hands, it still has a life form. God owns the root, and your power source is the owner of heaven, with all rights to produce any miracle that you will ever need. Also, as long as God is the root, then why are you worried? It is going to grow; you do not have to water it because God is going to water it with His increase. Just as the seeds are sown, your ground has already begun the tilling process, and seed cannot sit but so long. After your seed takes ground root, no matter what seed you sewed, it shall spring forth. Notice as the buds sprout their way out of the ground it will burst forth and then burst through. Now, you won't be able to see that day as it broke through the ground. You may look one day and still see no bud coming forth, but if you look again, you'll see the bud sitting right there. It snuck its way through while you weren't looking. Everything that you have sowed through your effort, through your will power, through your determination, and through your diligent work - God will direct an order per seed you have sown. All seeds must burst through; all seeds have time to grow so be patient as your seeds grow. God wants you to have all new fruit in your life. The Anointing Powers that are in Your Hands are going to produce new fruit in your life. Are you ready?

Most people look for the judgment as a bad thing, but from God fearing believers we shall receive a righteous reward. God will judge you for everything that you did right. He will set an everlasting promise with you that will be made according to what He decides you deserve.

I believe God for the covenant that He has made in my life. I want my promises and the land it sits on to flow with milk and honey. God's promises are true. God loves to be satisfied with good works, and as you please God with the Works of Your Hands, He will allow you more favor. He will fulfill His promises to you. The more you satisfy Him, the more power you will receive; He will give you larger works to do. God is a God of increase, a God of faithfulness and a God that will establish excellent works. As you prove to Him that you are faithful in your divine assignment, He will fulfill your vision to be large. Jesus will grant you every real reward because He has accepted your work with gladness in His heart. It is a beautiful thing when we satisfy God because He fulfills our every need and He will not rest until He accurately meets you.

Isaiah 61:11 says, For as the earth bringeth forth her bud, and as the garden causeth the things that are sown in it to spring forth; so the Lord GOD will cause righteousness and praise to spring forth before all the nations.

I pray that this book has brought you to your "ACCEPTABLE YEAR OF THE LORD" and that it has been more than you ever expected it to be in your life. In this is the year to expect things you've only dreamed of to appear in your life. It is valuable that you work with the Anointing Powers that God has given you. Utilize your gifts and keep them covered. There are many accomplishments by the works of your hands and the vision(s) that God has assigned unto you. I believe in The Anointing Powers of God and that no hands can accomplish a greater work without The Anointing. Keep in mind that every seed that you have sown, through your job ethic, effort, self-will, monetary, and so on that God is going to release your ground with the buds of all of your sown seeds. Some seeds you may have forgotten that you sowed and not all you can count. Just let God do the calculations while you send up your praises. Very soon it is all going to make men as well as you say; we serve an AWESOME GOD. The hands of the Lord are upon you, and the Anointing Powers Are in your Hands. Use them for His Glory and He shall bless your gift(s) as He shall receive greater glory. Praise Him for He is Worthy and Praise Him for all your buds springing forth fruit in your land of increase. Rejoice, because this is Your Acceptable Year of The Lord. Though many things in your life seemed to be empty, God is going to fulfill them all. Yes, this is your year where you shall gain favorable increase, so rejoice and be glad.

One night as I was talking to my aunt Pauline, we were discussing happiness. At that time, I had so many wrong things going on in my life, until I forgot all about being happy. I was trying hard to make everyone else happy until I forgot about myself. Through our conversation, she said, "Baby have you ever prayed for happiness." I thought for a minute, and I realized I wanted to be happy, but I never desired to be happy. It hit me from that day forward. As I thought more and more about happiness, I realized I thought of some things that would make me happy. My happiness was not in things because things can't love you back. You know sometimes we can believe that if God blesses us with something that we have wanted, that it will make us happy. Well, that is not true. Because as soon as you get it, the newness will fade away and then you will find yourself starting over and over again wanting something else. I thought of many things that would make me happy, but it was the one thing that God had given me, that truly caused my happiness. This gift contains joy late in the midnight hour, more valuable than gold, the brightest light that will never dim, dominion with all power; nothing will ever top this gift. It is too useful to price, and not everyone can receive it though it is one of a kind. It is the largest, most beautiful and powerful gift you will ever receive, and He wants your appreciation. In this gift, there is power to conquer your beginning and end. Jesus is the light in your darkest hours, and life for eternity. Though His gift took many years to develop, it's still growing today through our faith, as we grow stronger in the Lord. Know that Jesus paid the ultimate price. On the cross when He commended Himself to God, He Gave JEHOVAH all that He had and for that only JEHOVAH gave Him All Power. Jesus always showed great Honor towards His Heavenly Father. Just as Jesus rose up, you can too with your Precious Gift from God, through the

Blood of Jesus the Christ. He is your Opportunity to the tree of Life. Utilize your gift, and use this opportunity to gain the greatest life you can. Excellent life opportunity is in using your gift so, therefore, take advantage of it. Be blessed, be a praiser and become a victorious warrior. Remember, whatever you desire, whatever you seek after is what you will find. So, therefore, seek after the heart of Jesus and watch how He will ultimately bless your life. Also, note, your destiny is packed in your gift, so unwrap it and show it to the world.

A Prayer for You to Gain the Anointing

Our Heavenly Father that is full of righteousness, complete of mercy and grace - please Anoint the Works of my hands. Forgive my heart of all my wrong doings, Oh, Heavenly Father, make me right. Give me The Right Spirit that will make me good, allow the love of Jesus to cleanse my heart and make me pure. Keep me daily away from all temptations and strengthen me greater as I kneel in prayer. Allow my voice to sing acceptable praises unto you that will make me fall deeper in love with you. Teach me your secrets Lord; withhold no good thing from me. Though Lord I can't depend on myself, surely I will look towards the hills where my help comes. Jesus teaches me how to trust Him. Work that I must do, make it right to me. Anoint me Lord; anoint my head with your precious Holy Oil. Allow all the angels in heaven to pray for me, and touch my enemies and make them flee. Anoint me Lord; give me the power over all of my enemies. Give me strength in every weakness, Lord Anoint Me with your glory. Teach me, Lord, be my guide, lead me, Lord, guide my feet, lay your hands upon me. In the name of Jesus, I pray this Prayer, give me an answer Lord that you have responded to this prayer, and as you anoint me Bless Me to be that eternal blessing for your Glory so that many will see that you are JEHOVAH -

JIREH, and they will desire to please your heart. Allow this gift that you have given me to be your inspiration, teach me Lord how to inspire you; teach me how to love and encourage you - so that I can inspire millions and lead them all to you.

AMEN, AMEN & AMEN

Proverbs 10:22 says, The Blessings of the Lord, it maketh rich, and he addeth no sorrow with it.

My Personal Testimony

One day the Lord spoke to me. He told me so many beautiful things. I just laughed. For many of years, the enemy has tried to keep me from receiving all those wonderful things that The Lord told me. He has attacked me from every angle in my life, but God spared me to be a living witness. So that I can be fruitful and multiplied. So, therefore, His glory can reveal. I write because He fills my heart, I sing because He makes me happy and I am a believer because He has been my Life Instructor. When you want to become more than a conqueror, you will not let doubt, emburrassment, being a failure, a bruise, hurt, shame, sin or anything stop you from receiving your rewards. He can only award those that run their race. He has a way of bringing forth our blessings, and they are wrapped in our gifts. Open your gifts, use them until you reach your destiny.

Our Destiny is not for us, but by us.

~Barack Obama

The Exit Thought:

Often we do not even realize the value of our gifts. God gives us gifts as a remembrance of something supernaturally special. Regardless of the occasion or even if we don't always deserve them. He still finds a particular reason to give us gifts. The majority of the times we don't even appreciate them. Every gift is to Glorify God. His contributions represent just how powerful He is, who He is and that He is. Have you ever received a gift, and didn't even say thank you or failed to realize how special that gift was? Soon afterward, the person that gave you that particular gift - feelings were hurt, because they noticed that you didn't even take the time to appreciate it. There are a reason and something special behind every gift that you have received in your lifetime or given. To others, it may not have cost a lot of money, but truly it was special to them. Think for a moment when you have been low on funds, and you go out of your way to present a gift to someone, and they don't even take the time to appreciate it. However, to you, it was all you had, and you went out of your way. Surely, you could have kept your money and not even showed up for the occasion, but you did. I believe we make God feel that same way many of times, by not appreciating our gifts. God has gifted you with something unique that money just can't buy. His Son paid an ultimate cost of His Precious Blood, just for God to please you. What more can you ask for? Prove to God how much you appreciate your gift and inspire Him!

Proverbs 10:22 says, The Blessings of the Lord, it maketh rich, and he addeth no sorrow with it. As soon as you appreciate the gift(s) that God has given you, then you will begin to adore all of your prosperity possibilities. Eventually, He will give you the vision to incorporate your gift. Make Jesus proud, and He will make you happy. Use what He has given you, and you will receive His blessings. Your contributions will significantly cause you to prosper. Remember, and Jesus deserves His Glory, so, therefore, Give It to Him.

Be Richly Blessed, In Jesus Name.

Philippians 2:2 says, Fulfill ye my joy that ye be like minded, having the same love, being of one accord, of one mind; of mighty works that will fill you with joy and that will allow a multitude to also rejoice in it after the finishing of it.

Acknowledgments

JESUS – No other can take your place, I love you.

Bishop L. D. Parker – God works wonders my love.

Hattie Culp, Mom - You are the greatest.

Parielle, Larry, Marquel – You are my bundles of joy.

Dee Dee, Marianna, Mary – Sisters of love.

The H. O. T. Team for JESUS

Fountain of Life Publisher's House

Dr. Lincoln C. Lee & Silvermount Baptist

Church – Thanks for everything!

Patricia A Smith, thanks for being there when you know I needed a friend, you are God sent!

A Host of Aunts, Uncles & family – I love You All!

To all that I didn't list, I thank you too. Many have blessed my life knowingly and unknowingly – my heart says thanks.

Life is a terrible thing to waste and time is irreplaceable.

Powerful Inspiring books by Parice Parker

Living Life in A Messed Up Situation

Volume One

Living Life in A Messed Up Situation

Volume Two

Aggravated Assault on Your Mind

A Precious Gift from God

Word Wonders

The Anointing Powers of Your Hands

From Eating Crumbs to Transforming Wealth

The Birth of an Author Shall Be Born

Live Love Laugh & Be Happy

Power to Push You You

Visit Our Online Book Store or Where Ever Books Are Sold

www.pariceparker.biz

Aggravated Assault On Your Mind

Phenomenal: Have you ever felt, the very person you have surely loved or believed in has attacked you? It may have been your closest friend, relative, child, your spouse or even yourself. Sometimes you wanted to cry and could not. Shortly afterwards, while gazing about the pain immediately tears began to fall as a flowing river. Your heart has been assaulted and snared with claws of intentions to kill. A multitude of thoughts circulate in your mind and then you began to say to yourself **"How did I let this happen to me?"** Your situation was bound to occur, because somewhere along the way you have allowed your circumstance to control your mind. Allegedly, you put your trust in the wrong one or thing and then you are thrown off guard. Most definitely, you wonder, who do I blame? You did not realize you have entrusted so much of your heart to be assaulted through the passion of love you have given. A since of blindness has overwhelmed your thinking ability, rearranging your life, and throwing it off balance. Truly, there is an explanation and an apology due, but none is ever given. Certainly, you have tried to generate an effectual change. Perhaps, the more you have tried, the more your relationship seemed to die. **Instantly thinking, What Is The Use?**

A Precious Gift from God

Talent Is Too Good To Waste

Parice C Parker

Your Gift Discovery? It teaches one the value of their natural born talent and motivates one to Live Life On Purpose! This book inspires the heart, gives courage to your ***How to Ability*** and causes you to live in the pursuit of your happiness. Every natural born leader needs to read this book, it is **AWE – INSPIRING!**

Living Life In A Messed Up Situation

Volume One

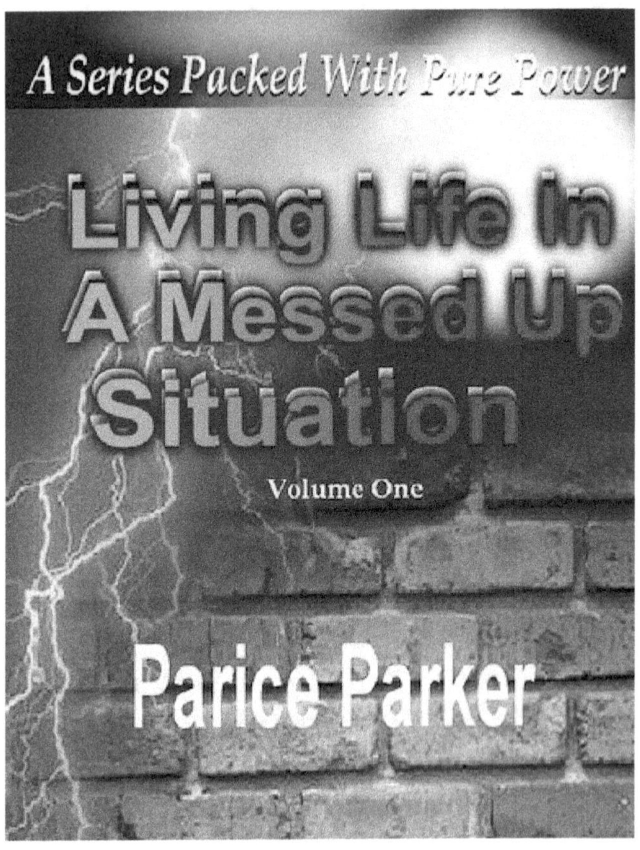

Powerful: God will assign the most in-depth spiritual cleaning service through the Blood of Jesus the Christ to clean up your messed up life. **Every messed up situation that you are living** in will have a **Sparkling Effect** when God gets finished with you. Some things He dusts off, others He wipes down and some need to be polished to shine. **Get Polished Perfect** after reading this book and simply gain it all.

The Birth of An Author Shall Be Born

Fascinating ... Dazing at the fact you have a book inside and don't know where to start or how to get it out! This book have dynamic key points and great strategies on how to succeed in book writing from start to finish. It's time to discover the author in you and to **GET THAT BOOK OUT Of YOU!** This book is full of techniques to motivate the author inside... The Birth of an Author Shall Be Born, Is It YOU?

Word Wonders

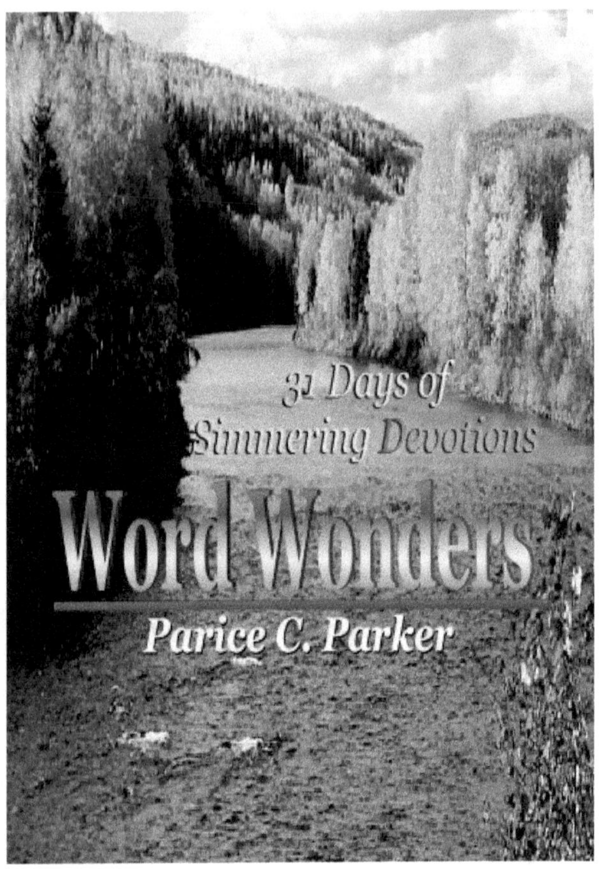

A Eye – Opening ... Word Wonder inspires your HOPE to Greatly Influence your FAITH and it's a magnificent daily devotional book to help keep you focused in word. It EMPOWERS Positive Powers to cause DIVINE FAVOR to ABOUND TOWARDS YOU! Simple things you need to be equipped with more favor from on high. Get This Book TODAY!

From Eating Crumbs To Transforming Wealth

Riveting … Finally, a book that keeps you in a thriving mental state that causes your HOPE to burst through! Now, it is time to identify the real you by introducing the TROPHY that is Hidden inside. It's your time to stop eating the crumbs of life and Indulge In Your WEALTHY Place!

The Anointing Powers of Your Hands

Do It, Doing It! Now, It's DONE! …

Parice C. Parker

Absorbing … The Anointing Powers of Your Hands has the ability to cause you to ***REACH*** for Dreams even You Thought They Were Impossible! It Motivates that **IMPOSSIBLE VISION TO COME TO PASS** and it places it in your **Rear View Mirror**!

Power to Push You

Military Force … When you fix your mind on the power to excel and purpose to hit the target, then it is a done deal. Your goal is now to achieve. No one, nothing or tiredness could stop you now. Power to Push You is missioned to cause you to be an eye specialist. Your eyes will begin to see the benefits of vision; the aspirations once accomplished, and you will have an **IMPEMTUOUS ZEAL.** No one can dream for this vision as you or push it in the manner you can and stay focused as you. Vision is the power to drive people but first one must see the fullness, must feel the passion for it to live and have an **IMPEMTUOUS ZEAL** to birth it. Vision is a life modifier and life decorator. It can give you a complete makeover from inside out. Also, when others see it, they will want to be a part or some of what you have. Your success will cause others to desire a much better life and give others a fresh hope to accomplish. Power to Push You speaks for itself and all that connects and read Power to Push You shall cause their visions to exist. It's a **DYNOMITE PUSHER!**

Life is a terrible thing to waste and time is irreplaceable.

Live Love Laugh & Be Happy

Live Love Laugh & Be Happy ***Fabulous*** **...** Daily many live life being terribly unhappy wanting others to really care but, are too often overlooked. It's time you get a new ray of hope. A time for healing inside and out. Live Love Laugh & Be Happy is purposed to expose new life to your everyday living. Your laughter is on its way, because those that sow in tears of sorrow, shall reap in tears of joy!

Life is a terrible thing to waste and time is irreplaceable.

Fountain of Life Publishers House

P. O. Box 922612, Norcross, GA 30010
Phone: 404.936.3989

For book orders or wholesale distribution

Website: www.pariceparker.biz

Life is a terrible thing to waste and time is irreplaceable.

www.ingramcontent.com/pod-product-compliance
Lightning Source LLC
LaVergne TN
LVHW012333100826
845148LV00017B/2282
9780978716257